Everyone can coach a pocket passer

QB or teach themselves to become a

pocket passer using the drills

I have described in this book.

Just follow my training philosophy:

Training Philosophy

Do each repetition **right**.....
do each repetition with **intensity**....
or.....
do each repetition **again**.

Coach Bill Renner

Coaching Note

I have used this QB pocket passer drill sequence with the QB's who played on my HS teams to:

- Coach and develop two Elite 11 National Ranked Top 5 HS QB's in the country
- Coach 3 consecutive QB's who have gone on full-scholarships to Division 1 schools and started there
- 4 QB's in 2 states that have over 25 state top ten records
- A QB who set the all-time state record for most yards in a single season
- 4 different QB's who averaged over 3,000+ yards and 28 passing TD's in a season for 10 years
- QB's who lead their teams to the state playoffs 6 out of 7 years straight

1

"The pocket passer Quarterback affects all the players on the defense. He can attack any defender at any time with his offensive weapons."

Coach Bill Renner

Drill Sequencing
For Skill Perfection and Correction

This drill sequence covers all the pocket movement skills a QB needs to be a successful pocket passer.

Strive to master the physical and mental mechanics of each drill. Then you will be prepared to execute them on game day.

The benefit of such a complete sequence is that any technique error you make can be traced back to one of these drills.

Then, you can go back and do that specific drill to fix that technique.

This gives you the ability to control how good you become. Because:

"if you can do the <u>drill</u>, you can do the <u>skill</u>."

Coach Bill Renner

Pocket Passer Quarterback Drill Sequence

Dominant Drop Drill
Quarterback Pocket Drill 1
*drop back body mechanics

Non-Dominant Drop Drill
Quarterback Pocket Drill 2
*counter balance drop back muscles

Swivel Hips Drop Drill
Quarterback Pocket Drill 3
*first step escape quickness

Drop-Run Drill
Quarterback Pocket Drill 4
*blitz unblocked off the edge

M Drill
Quarterback Pocket Drill 5
*pocket patience for non-rhythmic throws

3-Step Wide Base Drill
Quarterback Pocket Drill 6
*pocket balance and pocket patience

5-Step Wide Base Drill
Quarterback Pocket Drill 7
*pocket balance and pocket patience

Avoid-Shuffle Up Drill
Quarterback Pocket Drill 8
*5 technique, DE, up-the-field

Avoid-Reset Drill
Quarterback Pocket Drill 9
*3/0 technique, DT, up-the-middle with edge sealed
*blitz up-the-middle unblocked

Circle Target Drill
Quarterback Pocket Drill 10
*route progression memorization

Get It Out of Your Hand Drill
Quarterback Pocket Drill 11
*throwing WR quick screens

Dominant Drop Drill

Quarterback Pocket Passer Drill 1
drop back body mechanics

Purpose: to develop upper body drop back balance
to develop upper body drop back position
to develop proper drop back footwork
to develop drop back specific muscles

Dominant Drill Setup
Use a line that extends 30-35 yards.

Stance
Stand with your feet straddling the
line that runs across the field.
Assume the stance you would use
to take a snap from the center.
Hold a ball in your hands

First Step-TurnStep
Push off your left foot and step
back to the left side of the line with
your right foot. *(reverse this if you are
a left-handed quarterback)*

Think about stepping at the 7 position on a clock. The 6 would
be right behind you. Turn to
normal, dominant, drop back
side.

Second Step-Crossover Step
Take a 6-8 inch crossover step
with your left foot to begin the
movement backward. Step on
the line with this crossover
step.

This step is just 6-8 inches
past your turn step. It is not a
big step. It is short and quick.

7 o'clock   2nd Step
Turn Step   Crossover
Step

5

The drop back movement backward <u>is not</u> initiated with the upper body tilting backward

The <u>upper body</u> needs to remain <u>upright</u> and <u>stable</u> and with the <u>shoulders slightly open</u>, as in your pre-movement alignment, as you crossover step backward.

<u>There is no compromise in this upper body stability technique</u>.

Dominant Drop

Continue the drop back using the turn and crossover step until you have gone 30-35 yards. Your <u>crossover step</u> should be <u>on the line</u> the whole time. Your <u>turn step</u> is to the <u>left of the line</u> for the entire drop. Do not veer to the left or right side of the line, <u>stay on the line the whole time</u>.

To help you drop straight back on the line, <u>think about keeping your chin right on top of the line</u>. This keeps your front shoulder to the left of the line. <u>Don't look down to find the line</u>. Keep your <u>eyes straight ahead at the point on the line where you started</u>. This simulates looking down the field at the defense.

Notice: ➡

- ➢ Upper body tall
- ➢ Eyes like lasers on starting point
- ➢ Crossover foot on line
- ➢ Turn step left of the line
- ➢ Front shoulder open
- ➢ Ball on back breast plate

Ball Position in Dominant Drop
The ball is positioned on the back breastplate. It is between the back armpit and the sternum. No lower than the bottom of the breast and no higher than the collarbone.

The nose of the ball is tilted slightly up. It does not point at the ground. This tilt presets the cock of the wrist in the right release position.

As you move backward, you can rock the ball from the sternum to the armpit. Do not do this violently. Let your lower body move you backward. Rock the ball softly in rhythm with your footwork.

Coaching Notes
You must learn to have a balanced, upright and stable upper body as you drop back. Your lower body moves you backward while your upper body remains stationary. This allows your head and eyes to be stable while you look at the defense on your drop back.

Repetition Sequence
Do this drill down a line for 30-35 yards. Then turn around and do this drill back down the same line to your initial starting point. This is 2 times doing the drill for 30-35 yards each.

Dominant Drop Drill Execution Goal
Do it **RIGHT**….. Do it with **INTENSITY**…..

Do the Dominant Drop Back Drill at a speed where you can hold your upper body in the right position. If you have to go slower at first that is fine. Work to get to full speed drop back with a tall and stable upper body.

Non-Dominant Drop Drill
Quarterback Pocket Passer Drill 2
counter balance drop back muscles

Purpose: to develop upper body drop back balance
to develop upper body drop back position
to develop proper drop back footwork
to develop drop back specific muscles

Non-Dominant Drill Setup
Use a line that extends 30-35 yards.

Stance
Stand with your feet straddling
the line that runs across the field.
Assume the stance you would
use to take a snap from the
center. Hold a ball in your hands.

First Step-TurnStep
Push off your right foot and step
back to the right side of the line
with your left foot. *(reverse this if
you are a left-handed quarterback)*
Think about stepping at the 5
position on a clock. The 6 would be
right behind you. Turn to the
opposite side of your normal drop,
your non-dominant drop back side.

Second Step-Crossover Step
Take a 6-8 inch crossover step with
your right foot to begin the
movement backward.

5 o'clock
Turn Step

Step on the line with this crossover step. This
step is just 6-8 inches past your turn step. It is
not a big step. It is short and quick.

2nd Step
Crossover Step ⇨

8

The drop back movement backward <u>is not</u> initiated with the upper body tilting backward

The <u>upper body</u> needs to remain <u>upright</u> and <u>stable</u> and with the <u>shoulders slightly open</u>, as in your pre-movement alignment, as you crossover step backward.

<u>There is no compromise in this upper body stability technique</u>.

Non-Dominant Drop

Continue the non-dominant drop back using the turn and crossover step until you have gone 30-35 yards. Your <u>crossover step</u> should be <u>on the line</u> the whole time. Your <u>turn step</u> is to the <u>right of the line</u> for the entire drop. Do not veer to the left or right side of the line, <u>stay on the line the whole time</u>.

To help you drop straight back on the line, <u>think about keeping your chin right on top of the line</u>. This keeps your front shoulder to the right of the line. <u>Don't look down to find the line</u>. Keep your <u>eyes straight ahead at the point on the line where you started</u>. This simulates looking down the field at the defense.

<u>Notice:</u>
- ➢ Upper body tall
- ➢ Eyes like lasers on starting point
- ➢ Crossover foot on line
- ➢ Turn step left of the line
- ➢ Front shoulder open
- ➢ Ball on back breast plate

9

Ball Position in Non-Dominant Drop

The ball is positioned on the back breastplate. It is between the back armpit and the sternum. No lower than the bottom of the breast and no higher than the collarbone.

***ball is lower than desired here
*nose of ball needs to be tilted up more**

The nose of the ball is tilted slightly up. It does not point at the ground. This tilt presets the cock of the wrist in the right release position.

As you move backward, you can rock the ball from the sternum to the armpit. Do not do this violently. Let your lower body move you backward. Rock the ball softly in rhythm with your footwork.

Coaching Notes
You must learn to have a balanced, upright and stable upper body as you drop back even in the non-dominant position. Your lower body moves you backward while your upper body remains stationary. This allows your head and eyes to be stable while you look at the defense on your drop back.

Repetition Sequence
Do this drill down a line for 30-35 yards. Then turn around and do this drill back down the same line to your initial starting point. This is 2 times doing the drill for 30-35 yards each.

Non-Dominant Drop Drill Execution Goal
Do it **RIGHT**….. Do it with **INTENSITY**…..

Do the Non-Dominant Drop Back Drill at a speed where you can hold your upper body in the right position. If you have to go slower at first that is fine. Work to get to full speed drop back with a tall and stable upper body.

Swivel Hips Drop Drill
Quarterback Pocket Passer Drill 3
first step escape quickness

Purpose: to develop pocket movement patience
              to develop pocket escape footwork technique
              to develop pocket stance strength and balance

Swivel Hips Drill Setup
Use a line that extends 30-35 yards.

Stance
Stand with your feet straddling the line that runs across the field. Assume the stance you would use to take a snap from the center. Hold a ball in your hands

First Step-TurnStep
Push off your left foot and step back to the <u>left side of the line</u> with your right foot. *(reverse this if you are a left-handed quarterback)* Think about stepping at the <u>7 position on a clock</u>. The 6 would be right behind you. Turn to your normal, dominant, drop back side.

Second Step-Crossover Step
Take a 6-8 inch crossover step with your left foot to begin the movement backward. <u>Step on the line with this crossover step.</u>

This step is just 6-8 inches past your turn step. It is <u>not</u> a big step. It is short and quick.

7 o'clock
Turn Step   **2nd Step**
                    Crossover
                    Step

11

 The drop back movement backward is not initiated with the upper body tilting backward

The upper body needs to remain upright and stable and with the shoulders slightly open, as in your pre-movement alignment, as you crossover step backward.

There is no compromise in this upper body stability technique.

Swivel Hips Drop

Continue the dominant drop back using the turn and crossover step until you have taken 5 dominant drop steps.

On the 5th step, pivot, swivel your hips and turn to the non-dominant side.

Take 5 non-dominant drop steps using the turn and crossover steps. On the 5th step, pivot, swivel your hips and turn back to the dominant side.

When you turn to the dominant side this time, tuck the ball and turn and run forward through the last part of the 30-35 yards.

Head and Eyes Position

To help you drop straight back on the line, think about keeping your chin right on top of the line. This keeps your front shoulder to the left of the line.

Don't look down to find the line. Keep your eyes straight ahead at the point on the line where you started. This simulates looking down the field at the defense.

Swivel Hips Movement Sequence

Dominant

**Swivel Hips
to Non-Dominant**

Non-Dominant

**Swivel Hips
To Tuck and Run**

Tuck and Run

Ball Position in Swivel Hips Drop
The ball is positioned on the back breastplate. It is between the back armpit and the sternum. No lower than the bottom of the breast and no higher than the collarbone.

The nose of the ball is tilted slightly up. It does not point at the ground. This tilt presets the cock of the wrist in the right release position.

As you move backward, you can rock the ball from the sternum to the armpit. Do not do this violently. Let your lower body move you backward. Rock the ball softly in rhythm with your footwork.

Coaching Notes
You must learn to have a balanced, upright and stable upper body as you drop back. Your lower body moves you backward while your upper body remains stationary. This allows your head and eyes to be stable while you look at the defense on your drop back.

Repetition Sequence
Do this drill down a line for 30-35 yards. Then turn around and do this drill back down the same line to your initial starting point. This is 2 times doing the drill for 30-35 yards each.

Swivel Hips Drill Execution Goal
Do it **RIGHT**..... Do it with **INTENSITY**.....

Do the Swivel Hips Drill at a speed where you can hold your upper body in the right position. If you have to go slower at first that is fine. Work to get to full speed drop back with a tall and stable upper body.

M Drill
Quarterback Pocket Passer Drill 4
*pocket patience for non-rhythmic throws

Purpose: to develop wide base technique
to develop non-rhythm pocket footwork
to develop strength in the pocket stance position
to develop mental patience to stay in the pocket

M Drill Setup
Set up 5 cones in a 4 yard square with one cone in the middle of one of the sides. It looks like an "M" if you connected the cones.

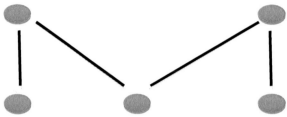

Starting Stance
Stand with your feet slightly wider than shoulder width. Establish an athletic base with knees bent over toes, upper body tall and weight evenly distributed on the toes. Hold the ball in pre-drop back position

Starting the Drill
Start in the lower right hand corner of the "M". Face forward in the first step turn position from your stance, front shoulder open, front foot open, tall upper body, wide base, athletic position.

starting position

Moving Through the "M"

In your stance, start <u>bouncing on your toes</u> keeping your wide base in the same position as you bounce. Without narrowing your base, moving your feet closer together, start moving backward toward the cone in the top right corner of the "M". Do not close off your front shoulder. Keep your head up and eyes looking forward.

starting cone

When you reach the top right cone, bounce downward toward the middle cone in the bottom of the "M". Then bounce backward at an angle to the top left corner of the "M". The final track is to the bottom left corner of the "M". See the pattern above.

The key is to stay in the athletic position with your front shoulder open, eyes up and ball in pre-throw position the entire time you are moving through the "M".

This "M" drill is where you develop the patience to not leave the pocket and run when you feel pressure.

Same athletic position halfway through M drill

16

Bouncing on your toes prepares you for a quick release.
You can plant, push and throw faster when your receiver comes open moving your feet like this.

Coaching Notes
You must learn to have a balanced, upright and stable upper body with a wide base as you stand in the pocket.   You need to have a pocket movement technique to use if a receiver is not open when you hit the top of your drop, or when you have to hold the ball for whatever reason. Staying in the pocket and not taking off and running is a mindset. This "M" drill teaches you pocket patience with a proper base.

Repetition Sequence
Do this drill from the right hand bottom corner through the "M" to the left hand bottom corner. Take a 30 second break and return by starting at the left hand bottom corner and bounce through the "M" to the right hand bottom corner. These two tracks are all you need to do.

Dominant Drop Drill Execution Goal
Do it **RIGHT**….. Do it with **INTENSITY**…..

Do the Dominant Drop Back Drill at a speed where you can hold your upper body in the right position.   If you have to go slower at first that is fine. Work to get to full speed drop back with a tall and stable upper body.

3-Step Wide Base Drill
Quarterback Pocket Drill 6
*pocket balance and pocket patience

Purpose: to develop wide base technique
to develop non-rhythm pocket footwork
to develop strength in the pocket stance position
to develop mental patience to stay in the pocket

3-Step Wide Base Setup
Set up in an under center stance. Head up, feet slightly wider than shoulder width apart, feet can be staggered, arms extended, butt of hands touching with palms facing each other to receive a simulated snap.

Starting the Drill
Once you are in your stance, use a single syllable of "Set Hut" and give the command to snap the ball.

starting position

As soon as the ball hits your hands take 3 steps to set up in your wide base throwing stance. The first step is a turn step to your dominant side, the second step is a crossover step the third step is a balance step. Stop on the third step and setup in a wide base.

Turn Step	**Crossover Step**	**Balance Step**

3-Step Wide Base Pocket Movement

As soon as you hit your third step, come to balance and hold yourself in this position for 3 seconds. This isometric position strengthens your body and calms your mind to be comfortable in the pocket.

Quarterback who has come to balance

Coaching Notes

You must learn to drop back and come to balance as quickly as possible when you are under the center. Moving backward on a drop then being able to stop and throw is a necessary talent to have.

Being off-balance and tilting your upper body left or right, forward or backward either in your drop or at the top of the drop causes the throwing arm to start in different positions to throw every time.

Make sure the quarterback uses good drop back techniques. They need to do this drill with great intensity.

Repetition Sequence

Do this drill 5 times.

Dominant Drop Drill Execution Goal

Do it **RIGHT**….. Do it with **INTENSITY**…..

Do the 3-Step Wide Base Drill at a speed where you can hold your upper body in the right position. If you have to go slower at first that is fine. Work to get to full speed drop back with a tall and stable upper body.

5-Step Wide Base Drill
Quarterback Pocket Drill 6
*pocket balance and pocket patience

Purpose: to develop wide base technique
to develop non-rhythm pocket footwork
to develop strength in the pocket stance position
to develop mental patience to stay in the pocket

5-Step Wide Base Setup
Set up in an under center stance.
Head up, feet slightly wider than
shoulder width apart, feet can be
staggered, arms extended, butt of
hands touching with palms facing
each other to receive a simulated
snap.

Starting the Drill
Once you are in your stance, use
a single syllable of "Set Hut" and
give the command to snap the
ball.

starting position

As soon as the ball hits your hands take 5 steps to set up in
your wide base throwing stance. The first step is a turn step to
your dominant side, the second step is a crossover step the
third step is a balance step. Stop on the third step and setup
in a wide base.

Turn Step   **Crossover Step**   **Balance Step**

5-Step Wide Base Pocket Movement

As soon as you hit your fifth step, come to balance and hold yourself in this position for 3 seconds. This isometric position strengthens your body and calms your mind to be comfortable in the pocket.

Quarterback who has come to balance

Coaching Notes

You must learn to drop back and come to balance as quickly as possible when you are under the center. Moving backward on a drop then being able to stop and throw is a necessary talent to have.

Being off-balance and tilting your upper body left or right, forward or backward either in your drop or at the top of the drop causes the throwing arm to start in different positions to throw each time.

Make sure the quarterback uses good drop back techniques. They need to do this drill with great intensity.

Repetition Sequence

Do this drill 5 times.

Dominant Drop Drill Execution Goal

Do it **RIGHT**….. Do it with **INTENSITY**…..

Do the 5-Step Wide Base Drill at a speed where you can hold your upper body in the right position. If you have to go slower at first that is fine. Work to get to full speed drop back with a tall and stable upper body.

Avoid-Shuffle Up Drill
Quarterback Pocket Drill 8
*5 technique, DE, up-the-field

Purpose: to develop shuffle up in pocket movement
to develop mental cues to shuffle up in pocket
to develop strength to change pocket direction
to develop mental discipline to move in pocket

Avoid-Shuffle Up Setup
Set up in an under center stance. Head up, feet slightly wider than shoulder width apart, feet can be staggered, arms extended, butt of hands touching with palms facing each other to receive a simulated snap.

Set up a target to throw at. It can be a shield, tire or shirt mounted on a PVC frame.

Mount the object so that it is 5 feet high which is the height of a receivers chest and shoulders.

starting position

Shield   **Tire**   **Shirt**

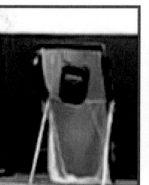

Starting the Drill

Once you are in your stance, use a <u>single syllable of "Set Hut"</u> and give the command to snap the ball.

As soon as the ball hits your hands <u>take 3 steps</u> to set up in your wide base throwing stance. The first step is a <u>turn step</u> to your dominant side, the second step is a <u>crossover step</u> the third step is <u>a balance step</u>. Stop on the third step and setup in a wide base.

Turn Step	Crossover Step	Balance Step

Avoid-Shuffle Up Pocket Movement

As soon as you hit your third step, drop your hips, plant your back foot, and aggressively push to shuffle up in the pocket for 3 shuffle steps. <u>Do not narrow your base to shuffle up</u>.

Keep your feet under your shoulders…..

then, reestablish your wide base
to throw from.

And, get the front foot down
as quickly as possible….

to prepare for a quick release.

Remember, the defensive ends are
coming up the field full speed and
you have to shuffle up in the pocket
to avoid them. Be quick with your movements!

Coaching Notes
You must learn to shuffle up in the pocket to avoid defensive ends that are coming at your drop position full speed.   In this scenario, they have beaten your offensive tackle(s) off the ball and you cannot set your feet at the top of your drop to throw.

Avoid Shuffle Up allows you to create vertical separation from the defensive ends to avoid them hitting or sacking you.

Your thoughts as you Shuffle Up are:
1) keep your front shoulder pointing down the field to be in throwing position
2) keep your eyes up and try to find your short route, check down, receiver
3) hold the ball securely so it does not get slapped out of your hands
4) be stable with the upper body but quick with the feet

Do this drill with great intensity. It is your part of your job to help the lineman out when they get beat.

Repetition Sequence
Do this drill 6 times.
Place the target in front of you for 2 throws. Place the target to your right side for 2 throws. Then, place the target to your left side for 2 throws.

Or, you can move and leave the target in the same place. But learn to shuffle up and throw to all sides.

Dominant Drop Drill Execution Goal
Do it **RIGHT**….. Do it with **INTENSITY**…..

Avoid-Reset Drill
Quarterback Pocket Drill 9
*Defensive Tackles, up-the-middle with edge sealed
*blitz up-the-middle unblocked

Purpose: to develop pocket escape movement techniques
to develop mental cues to escape the pocket
to develop movement reset-to-throw techniques
to develop mental discipline out-of-pocket throws

Avoid-Reset Setup

Set up in an under center stance. Head up, feet slightly wider than shoulder width apart, feet can be staggered, arms extended, butt of hands touching with palms facing each other to receive a simulated snap.

Set up a target to throw at. It can be a shield, tire or shirt mounted on a PVC frame.

Mount the object so that it is 5 feet high which is the height of a receivers chest and shoulders.

starting position

Shield	**Tire**	**Shirt**

28

Avoid-Reset Drill Setup
Place a cone 7 yards behind where you align under the center. Then place a cone 5 yards to either side of that cone only just 5 yards deep.

Starting the Drill
Once you are in your stance, use a <u>single syllable of "Set Hut"</u> and give the command to snap the ball.

As soon as the ball hits your hands <u>take 5 steps</u> to set up in your wide base throwing stance. The first step is a <u>turn step</u> to your dominant side, the second step is a <u>crossover step</u> the third step is <u>a balance step</u>. Stop on the fifth step and setup in a wide base.

Turn Step	Crossover Step	Balance Step

Avoid-Reset Pocket Movement

As soon as you hit your fifth step, come to balance in your wide base stance for 1 second. Then push off your back foot and sprint laterally to your left 5 yards to a cone.

5 Step Drop Avoid-Reset Left

Avoid-Reset is a 5 phase process:

1) 5-Step drop, come-to-balance at top of drop
2) Push to move lateral left or right
3) Lateral run
4) Flip your hips
5) Reset, come-to-balance, in your wide base

Top of drop	Push to move	Lateral Run

Flip the Hips   **Come back to Balance and Face Target**

Once you reset get your <u>front foot down quickly</u> and release the ball.

Avoid-Reset Pocket Movement
Repeat the avoid-reset pocket movement, only move laterally to your right to throw.

5 Step Drop Avoid-Reset Right

Coaching Notes
When you have defensive pressure up the middle, from a defensive tackle or linebacker, you must learn to move laterally to reestablish a pocket area to throw the ball.

In this scenario, the defensive tackles or blitzing linebacker has beaten your offensive guards) off the ball and you cannot set your feet at the top of your drop to throw.

Avoid-Rest allows you to create horizontal separation from the defensive tackles to avoid them hitting or sacking you.

Do this drill with great intensity. It is your part of your job to help the lineman out when they get beat.

Repetition Sequence
Do this drill 6 times. 3 times to the left and then 3 times through the right. Place the target 15 yards away from the center and 10 yards over from the center.

Dominant Drop Drill Execution Goal
Do it **RIGHT**….. Do it with **INTENSITY**…..

Circle Target Drill
Quarterback Pocket Drill 10
*route progression memorization

Purpose: to develop memorization skills
               to develop mental cues to find receivers
               to develop mental discipline to stand in the pocket
               to develop strength to stand in the pocket

Circle Target Setup
Align one cone in the center where the QB will stand. Put 4 other cones around him as seen in the layout below. The cones should be 10 yards from the QB.

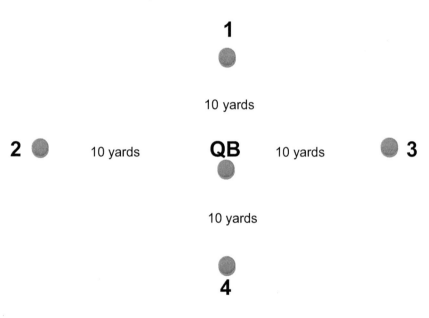

Put a receiver at each cone. They will be the number of the cone they are standing at 1, 2, 3 or 4.

The receiver must remember his number for the drill. When he hears his number called the QB is going to throw him the ball.

Starting the Drill
The QB will stand in the middle with a good wide base. He will bounce in a circle using the "M" drill technique. The QB must remember which receiver is which number.

Circle Target Drill Procedures
As the QB bounces in a circle, the coach will call out a number and the QB must turn to that receiver and throw him the ball. He needs to get turned to the receiver and get the ball out as fast as possible.

Have the QB bounce clockwise and counter clockwise in a controlled smooth rhythmic manner.

Coaching Notes
This drill creates mental anxiety for the QB. He wants to hear a number so he starts bouncing too fast in a circle. Watch for this and tell him to calm down mentally and don't anticipate when you are going to call a number. Just bounce and be calm.

The QB should keep his eyes level, his mind calm and think about where each number is as he bounces. Then when he hears the number he will get turned quicker. Clear mind, focused on mapping where the numbers are, will translate to knowing where his routes are on a play.

34

Get It Out of Your Hand Drill

Quarterback Pocket Drill 11
*throwing WR quick screens

Purpose: to develop memorization skills
to develop mental cues to find receivers
to develop mental discipline to stand in the pocket
to develop strength to stand in the pocket

Get It Out of Your Hand Setup

Align in the shotgun 5 yards from the snapper. Assume a tall, balanced athletic stance to receive the snap. Head up, eyes on the center, hands out front, feet shoulder width apart are all dynamics of the athletic stance.

Put a receiver or a target 15 yards from you and 1-2 yards behind the line of scrimmage like you are throwing a quick screen.

Get It Our of Your Hand Field Setup

You can use targets if you don't have receivers.

QB

WR	15 yards		15 yards	**WR**
⬤		**C**		⬤
2 yds behind C		⬤		2 yds behind C

35

<u>Starting the Drill –Throwing to the Left</u>
Take the snap from the center. Take a short step back with your right foot. Swing your left foot around to your wide base throwing position. As soon as it hits the ground, start the throwing process.

short step right foot

left foot back to balanced base

front foot on ground load and throw

Starting the Drill –Throwing to the Right

Take the snap from the center. Pivot on your left foot and swing your right foot back to the wide base throwing position. As soon as it hits the ground, start the throwing process.

pivot on left foot   **right foot planted at target**

Front foot down load and throw

Training Guidelines
For Pocket Passer QB Drills

Drill	Reps	Distance
Dominant Drop Drill Quarterback Pocket Drill 1	2	30-35 yards
Non-Dominant Drop Drill Quarterback Pocket Drill 2	2	30-35 yards
Swivel Hips Drop Drill Quarterback Pocket Drill 3	2	30-35 yards
Drop-Run Drill Quarterback Pocket Drill 4		1 clockwise 1 counter clockwise *3 times around the cone is 1 rep
M Drill Quarterback Pocket Drill 5		2 times through the cones
3-Step Wide Base Drill Quarterback Pocket Drill 6	5	3-step drops
5-Step Wide Base Drill Quarterback Pocket Drill 7	5	5-step drops
Avoid-Shuffle Up Drill Quarterback Pocket Drill 8	6	2 throw left 2 throw right 2 throw middle
Avoid-Reset Drill Quarterback Pocket Drill 9	6	3 throw left 3 throw right
Circle Target Drill Quarterback Pocket Drill 10	3	call out 3 numbers for one rep
Get It Out of Your Hand Drill Quarterback Pocket Drill 11	6	3 throw left 3 throw right

***Use this program to build good pocket movement
physical and mental skills**

"This drill sequence allows you to coach the physical and mental skills it takes for a QB to sit in the pocket and pass.

Focus on the mental cues that each drill incorporates to teach the QB what to do in the pocket."

Coach Bill Renner

For additional coaching
educational materials
by Coach Bill Renner
visit:

www.billrennerfootball.com

Made in the USA
Middletown, DE
08 March 2017